FABER NEW POET

IN THE SAME SERIES

Zaffar Kunial

FABER & FABER

First published in 2014
by Faber & Faber Ltd
Bloomsbury House
74–77 Great Russell Street
London WC1B 3DA

Typeset by Hamish Ironside
Printed in England by Abbeystar

ACKNOWLEDGEMENTS

With thanks to (among many others) the Poetry Society and
the judges of the National Poetry Competition, New Writing North
for the Northern Writers' Award, and the Wordsworth Trust for the
residency. 'Placeholder' was written for an exhibition, Wordsworth
and Bashō: Walking Poets, and its epigraph is from Seamus Heaney.

A CIP record for this book
is available from the British Library

ISBN 978-0-571-32122-3

2 4 6 8 10 9 7 5 3 1

Contents

The Word

I couldn't tell you now what possessed me
to shut summer out and stay in my room.
Or at least attempt to. In bed mostly.
It's my dad, standing in the door frame
not entering – but pausing to shape advice
that keeps coming back. 'Whatever is matter,

must *enjoy the life*.' He pronounced this twice.
And me, I heard wrongness in putting a *the*

before *life*. In two minds. Ashamed. Aware.
That I knew better, though was stuck inside
while the sun was out. That I'm native here.
In a halfway house. Like that sticking word.
That definite article, half right, half
wrong, still present between *enjoy* and *life*.

Placeholder

on frozen Windermere

Those old blades scratched the surface of Esthwaite
and not Windermere, as Heaney had it,
tracing that scrape with a star in 'Wordsworth's Skates'.
That the star lay elsewhere sits about right –
I like the mistake. The lake being astray
speaks of dark ice, like Wordsworth's crossings-
out – returning to fix the line that Heaney
must have had by heart:
                    To cut across the ——————
of a star. I've scored that space because *shadow*
first held sway. And wrongly, as light can't cast
dark. Next up, the star's *image* would land where
his skate passed. Then, the curt Latin, at last:
reflex. Fitting the foot.
                    And, beyond the grave,
that fixed word's meaning would still change the script.
Cold 'reflection' gave ground to a quick nerve –
till the star touched base, as the steel blade slipped
across that spot of ice – and scored deep space.
The slide in meaning fits this sliding place.

Hill Speak

There is no dictionary for my father's language.
His dialect, for a start, is difficult to name.
Even this taxi driver, who talks it, lacks the knowledge.
Some say it's Pahari – 'hill speak' –
others, Potwari, or Pahari-Potwari –
too earthy and scriptless to find a home in books.
This mountain speech is a low language. *Ours*. 'No good.
You should learn speak Urdu.' I'm getting the runaround.

Whatever it is, this talk, going back, did once have a script:
Landa, in the reign of the Buddhists.
. . . So was Dad's speech some kind of Dogri?
Is it Kashmiri? Mirpuri? The differences are lost on me.
I'm told it's part way towards Punjabi,
but what that tongue would call *tuwarda*,
Dad would agree was *tusaanda* –
'yours' –

truly, though there are many dictionaries for the tongue
   I speak,
it's the close-by things I'm lost to say;
things as pulsed and present as the back of this hand,
never mind stumbling towards some higher plane.
And, either way, even at the rare moment I get towards –
or, thank God, even getting to –
my point, I can't put into words
where I've arrived.

Butterfly Soup

This butterfly comes from a bud
they call the small cocoon
it occupied before it was
this speckled, flitting bloom.

Back in that darkly shrunken space
it breaks down cell by cell.
Now, liquefied, its black-holed eyes
gape past that pupal gel:

that dense and nascent universe
that spooled our sent-out star.
This point that bore that point before

flaps storms to Palomar.

Fielder

If I had to put my finger on where this started,
I'd trace a circle round the one moment I came to, or the one
that placed me, a fielder – just past the field, over the rope,
having chased a lost cause, leathered for six . . .
when, bumbling about, obscured in the bushes,
I completely stopped looking for the ball –
perhaps irresponsibly – slowed by bracken, caught by light
that slipped the dark cordon of rhododendron hands,
a world hidden from the batsmen, the umpires and my team,
like the thing itself: that small, seamed planet, shined
on one half, having reached its stop, out of the sphere of sight.
And when I reflect, here, from this undiscovered city,
well north of those boyish ambitions – for the county,
maybe later, the country – I know something of that minute
holds something of me, there, beyond the boundary,
in that edgeland of central England. A shady fingernail
of forest. The pitch it points at, or past, a stopped clock.
Still, in the middle, the keeper's gloves
clap at the evening. Still, a train clicks
on far-off tracks. And the stars are still to surface.
The whole field, meanwhile, waiting for me,
some astronaut, or lost explorer, to emerge with a wave
that brings the ball – like time itself – to hand. A world restored.
But what I'd come to find, in that late hour
was out of mind, and, the thing is, I didn't care
and this is what's throwing me now.

from Empty Words

Meaning 'homeland' – *mulk*
(in Kashmir) – exactly how
my son demands milk.

*

Full-rhyme with *Jhelum*,
the river nearest his home –
my father's 'realm'.

*

You can't put a leaf
between *written* and *oral*;
that first 'A', or *alif*.

*

Letters. West to east
Mum's hand would write; Dad's script goes
east to west. Received.

*

Invader, to some –
neither here nor there, with me –
our rhododendron.

*

Where migrating geese
pause to sleep – somewhere, halfway
is this pillow's crease.

*

Here we separate
for the first time, on our walk,
at the kissing-gate.

*

Old English 'Deor' –
an exile's lament, the past's
dark, half-opened door.

*

Yes, I know. *Empty*.
But there's just something between
the *p* and the *t*.

*

At home in Grasmere –
thin mountain paths have me back,
a boy in Kashmir.

And Farther Again

The motif 'Three Hares', each chasing the scut
of his dead spit in front, is tricky in terms
of provenance;

catchable as Scotch mist, or haars hunted at sea,
it's been traced to the Silk Road
and farther again,

tracked to the heels of the Sui Dynasty
as a hieroglyph, as it happens,
of the verb

'to be'. It's on Mongol metalwork and a coin
from Iran that just missed Rumi's
hand, dated 1281.

It's a Christian thing too, a sign of eternity
or the trinity; again, hard to nail down
or put an X exactly

where this began. Whether bossed at crossed vaults
in gothic churches, or inlaid in floors,
see how the three

rotating hares have ears in common; heads linked
in the round, like the dots that eye
the teardrops in the yin

and yang. And now our words are of China,
I put a 'Three Hares' tile into your hand –
a gift that finds

a void – like the gaps within the mould. But its old
circular theme, set inside a square,
gets me thinking of Escher,

how the far ground becomes the fore, a fugue
that little Zaphyr could trace
around and draw.

And as you're telling me that a nail won't get far
into the stone bricks above your door,
it brings up the three-

chaired counselling the two of us undertook;
how each hour was a strange loop
where split hairs went

back and forth, over a hook, a theme to our patterns,
the gaps in the listening, repeated
to no end. So

it's hard now to hear it, and from the mother of my son –
you put the tile down – *we can't get back*;
you've moved on.

On the Brief

I have a brief for a Valentine's card:
Short sentiment. No mention of love. Must sound familiar.
Piece of cake. A walk in the park.
But I'm stuck again. Someplace between
the briefs on the desk and leaves elsewhere;
between nine-to-five and spots of time;
the stars snowing through the screensaver

and the rain-clotted window.
And getting nowhere. Nothing doing. Again.
There's another poem I've half a mind
to begin, briefly. But instead,
much, too much time later . . . and with much . . .
it is written: *Can't get you out of my head.*

Spider Trees, Pakistan

During the early 1850s, it sometimes seemed as if the British and the Mughals lived not only in different mental worlds, but almost in different time zones.
– WILLIAM DALRYMPLE, *The Last Mughal*

English mists in subcontinental sun;
the withered veil at Miss Havisham's house;
think of that thought in the brain of John Donne
scrawling *In that the world's contracted thus*;
think of holding-spells catching up with time
the way snow floods the sky in slow suspension;
think, though it's a stretch, like shock-haired Einstein
wedding time and space as lacework tension . . .

With floods in Sindh, and their tenants long stranded,
the trees are warped globes, veiled spectres of silk.
It's these photos that have me – stretched, extended,
glued to a webpage since opening a link –
racking my brain for lines to catch how they carry
the gravities of home. Worlds I can't marry.

Us

If you ask me, *us* takes in *undulations* –
each wave in the sea, all insides compressed –
as if, from one coast, you could reach out to

the next; and maybe it's a Midlands thing
but when I was young, *us* equally meant *me*,
says the one, 'Oi, you, tell us where yer from';

and the way supporters share the one fate –
I, being one, am *Liverpool* no less –
cresting that Mexican wave: *we*, or *us*,

a shore-like state, two places at once – God
knows what's in it; and, at opposite ends,
my heart's sunk at separations of *us*.

When it comes to us, colour me unsure.
Something in me, or it, has failed the course.
I'd love to think I could stretch to it – us –

but the waves therein are too wide for words.
I hope you get, here, where I'm coming from.
I hope you're with me on this – between love

and loss – where I'd give myself away, stranded
on this single stress, us. I hope, from here on
out, I'll say it and not be too far wrong.

The Lyric Eye

Methinks I see these things with parted eye
– WILLIAM SHAKESPEARE, *A Midsummer Night's Dream*

I've stood at your portrait at different times.
Clocked my own face, now and then, in the glass.
A cloud, eclipsed. Vaguely before, or behind
you. Half cast. At a loss.
                              Even the gloss
back then, at school, left me looking this blank.
In the dark. Not on the same page as you.

But when I stand, here, almost in a blink
I can place my eyes – glazed over your stare;
let you lend me your ear, your famous cheek;
let the flare of your nostril stretch thin air;
even try on your earring, from five feet,
four centuries apart. I swear – by this lapse –
the light on your mouth seems cast
                                       half on mine
when I borrow the line between your lips.

Liquidity

Looking it up, my eyes slip further down the page
to one of the five entries of *list*:
'3 v. the tilt of a ship' – perhaps later to sink;
'. . . a variant of earlier *lust*'.

And since it's topical this week,
I think of that boating term, *bail out*. And Greece.
And slipperily, by way of its old colony
of Syracuse, or Sicily,
Archimedes . . .

Across the water (*Mare Nostrum*)
in Constantinople, on tenth-century goatskin, a parchment
of prayers was found at the turn of the last
century – a palimpsest
or overlaid double entry.

And when the prayers were wiped out, or made palest,
underwriting the higher ink
was the legendary (just legible) after-bath treatise:
'On Floating Bodies',

each raised letter, not Latin, but Greek –
in Archimedes' own priceless language –
another bonus, to say the least.

Even in translation, his treasury of theorems –
in fluid mechanics and displacement –
had been almost entirely
lost.

Q

Somewhere (thank you, father) over the hills,
through some trap-door in my mind, despite my having
no call to speak it, and hearing of it so long ago,
I know the Urdu *ishq* is love.
And further, how it's the highest (a divine fervour,
a bolt cued from the round heavens – almost angelic)
among a whole host of forms, or feathers, of love
like that myth of subtle Inuit measures of snow

and now I've *utterly gone and put my foot in it*
and other shoppers are turning round, as we inch
up to the queue's end, still far from those tills,
and she's prodding me to explain my short-falling
answer – giving the nod, when she asked me *If* . . . and *Whether* . . .
– she swears that at the end of my assent she heard me whisper
-*ish*

A Drink at the Door

As I had asked for a night-light, the chamberlain
had brought me in, before he left me, the good old
constitutional rush-light of those virtuous days . . .
– CHARLES DICKENS, *Great Expectations*

That's what I'm reading here. I mean the Dickens.
That and some downloaded contemporary
I keep switching from, on my close-lit Kindle.
But it's not the light that came with this reader
and candles the cold, framed screen; it's the trick
of the light in this pub that detains me.
And not in this place alone. What is it
this yellowed, well-thumbed light has borrowed from?
By a less lonely table, a dog's ear
twitches. Somehow the glow pooled round my pew
hosts its own table talk. As mahogany
is a wood of a certain age, so too
this light is dated, and in turn refracted
by the dark matter that's caked in the grain.
And it's refracted, beyond that, by smoke
at the back of this malt, death and life mixed,
as familiar as a browned penny,
particular as fog. And it picks up
a dim street in Dickens, a door that gives
to this light, refracted here by the din
and the sharp bark of that dog. The Bear.
That was it. Dad's early haunt. Those big doors
that looked locked. And there, ensconced, hours later,
the same filament in frosted, smoked glass.

*

Like a burr stuck in the folds of my scarf,
this light has trailed me longer than I knew.
Out there, the darkness also has a hand
in these refractions. That and the bitter
cold I'm in from. If I keep losing you,
please bear with the thought of light. Like this shot
of malt bears its long, peat finish, sea-noted, late . . .
There's a low fire breathing, and an argument
somewhere. And I've come to an inn. In Orkney,
1824. In his Irish burr,
I hear the landlord attempt to intervene.
Four generations later, his descendant
pokes at the grate of his pub in Aberdeen.
And his wayward daughter asks for a light
in a Midlands asylum, home for life.
And her daughter, between trains, wanders out
to Needless Alley, looks in at the Windsor,
catching the eye of my eventual father.
Shortly they'll see, in this same light, they share
the one brand of cigarette.
                                    These refractions
will go on, past my stay; I'm only here
for one. A drink at the door. A last drop
trails down the glass. I'll pack my Kindle away.
Exit this light that has taken me in.